THE
"KILL THE UMPIRE" HANDBOOK

101 Questions You'd Like to Ask the Umpire

Patrick M. Sullivan

M
P
MONTEZUMA
PUBLISHING

San Diego, CA

Published by Montezuma Publishing

Montezuma Publishing Aztec Shops Ltd.
San Diego State University
San Diego, California 92182-1701
Phone: 619-594-7552
email: Montezuma@aztecmail.com
Website: www.montezumapublishing.com

ISBN-10: 0-7442-3020-9
ISBN-13: 978-0-7442-3020-8

Publishing manager: Kim Mazyck
Cover design: Lia Dearborn
Cover photo: Sharon K. Karr Photography
Text formatting: Lia Dearborn
Production mastering: Jane Sanders
Quality control: Jacob Kalmonson

CONTENTS

III. The Pitcher 45

INTRODUCTION

To umpires of recreational baseball, fans—usually parents—can be anything from a pleasant distraction to a necessary evil.

They give their time to their budding superstar's mini-career by bringing them to and from games, working concessions, coaching, or just being fans in the stands—and that's all great.

When are they an "evil?" When they're verbally pelting us from the stands for a correct ruling. This is usually out of ignorance or in misguided "fun," but it's frustrating when it makes others think we messed up when we didn't. Most people in the stands have never even *seen* a rule book, much less *read* one.

Why don't we turn around and explain? I learned why in my first season, over forty years ago now. The risk of a shouting match is not worth the feeble hope of a teaching moment.

Yeah, I've been at this so long that when I started umpiring, they actually called us "ump"—now it's "blue"—and we wore blue from top to bottom. Except the belt and shoes, every part of our uniform in those days was a shade of blue—light blue shirt, navy slacks and (optional) jacket, navy cap, and navy ball bags. We went to gray slacks a year or two later, and that started us away from the color that produced the nickname fans still use.

Anyway, one day in my twenty-fourth season of calling amateur baseball, it occurred to me that any *fair-minded* spectator would be willing—even anxious—to know more about how we decide things. At least, I don't know many people who *want* to be wrong. But read a boring rule book?

Here's your chance to know what's *really* going on the next time somebody yells "Kill the umpire!"

ABOUT THIS HANDBOOK

1. It's about rules and calls, not coaching or strategy. Coaches also catch flak, but their issues are for another author.

2. Rules vary with age level and/or organization (The key revision in most pre-teen leagues, not allowing lead-offs, greatly changes base stealing and eliminates the hit-and-run play mentioned in Q&A 18.) Most youth programs up to and including American Legion base-ball use the Official Baseball Rules (OBR), which is the professional game's book, with various revisions. However, high school and major college baseball both have their own complete sets of rules. Schoolboy ball uses an independently written book we call "FED" because it is developed and published by the National Federation of State High School Associations; the FED book is more different from OBR than any rule book I know of, and I'll try to point out the import-

ant differences. While the National Collegiate Athletic Association (NCAA) rule book is also *not* an edited version of OBR, its content is much more similar than FED's. The smaller schools of the National Association of Intercollegiate Athletics (NAIA) *do* use OBR—again, with modifications. Given my experience and this handbook's target audience—parents of youth amateur players—you can figure I'm quoting OBR unless I specify otherwise. (Here's one: a team's field chief is the "manager" in OBR but the "coach" in FED and NCAA.) If you can't find something I've said in any rule book, please be aware I'm also drawing on classroom training, umpiring manuals, and *case* books.

3. Know that even experts are constantly learning baseball's rules. When I was a sixteen-year-old fan listening to my Reds play out in Los Angeles, Dodger Manny Mota tried to steal home in the bottom of the eleventh inning. Reds' play-by-play announcer Al Michaels—yes, the now long-time national network sportscaster—described the action as Johnny Bench tagged Mota to send us to a twelfth inning. Yet umpire Harry Wendelstedt then declared Mota safe, giving the Dodgers the winning run. It's fair to say Michaels went ballistic, as did I; but the next day, I thought with a cooler head. A *Major League* umpire ought to know what he's doing—in fact, this one would later operate an umpiring school that sent gradu-

ates to the pros—so I opened two things: my mind and a rule book. He was right! (Why? See Q&A 52.) I started umpiring the next season; more importantly, I'd learned that even a top-notch baseball man didn't know it all! Do you?

4. Fans and coaches never say umpires are perfect. Nor, in *normal* conversation, do they *say* we *should* be—but on any given play, they sure seem to *think* so. Look, we *all* miss calls. The *best* umpires aren't doing youth ball, but even the cream atop pro and college aren't *perfect*. I want to show you how a call that *seems* so wrong *may* be right. A side effect my colleagues may not like: you *will* better know when an ump *is* wrong. Just remember, your perception *must* be colored by team loyalty, *may* be based on myth, or *might seem* fair absent actual rules knowledge.*

5. This will be hard for some and common sense for others, but here it is, flat: if it doesn't make any difference, it doesn't make any difference. If some technicality doesn't impact a play, we'll ignore it and let them play. People, it's a *game*!

---

* See how *not* to umpire by watching "Out at the Old Ball Park," a 1960 episode of the television series *Have Gun – Will Travel*. Paladin employed this system, to the detriment of the game as well as the show!

That said, there are several plays in which close doesn't count:

- The batted ball was either fair or foul.
- The fly ball was or was not caught in the air.
- The pitch touched or didn't touch the bat or the batter.
- The ball touched or didn't touch dead-ball territory.
- The runner touched or didn't touch the base.

6. I've written these as questions and answers, as I remember or imagine such conversations. For quick reference, I've grouped them by which player participant likely brought you into these pages, duplicated and cross-referenced as I thought helpful. A list of questions serves as the table of contents.

I'd love to be calling a game some day and see somebody whip out a copy. There's a fan I would *gladly* talk with about a call—after the game is over, of course.

I. THE BATTER

1. What's the strike zone?

That space over home plate that's also between the bottom of a ready-to-swing batter's knees and a spot halfway between the top of the shoulders and the waistband (clothing being adjustable, I consider this the sternum). This pentahedron of air is seventeen inches by, on an adult, roughly three feet. Contrary to "Hey, blue, it's been that for a hundred years," the OBR zone has changed often and a lot: hittable, 1858–86 (Q&A 2); shoulders to knees, 1887–1949 and 1963–68; armpits to top of knees, 1950–62 and 1969–87. The current top of the zone arrived in 1988, but the bottom remained the top of the knees until 1996. (As of this writing, NCAA and FED use this but Little League® still uses armpits to bottom of knees.) The pitch must touch this zone *in flight*; if it bounces through there it is *not* a strike (Q&A 38).

2. Do umpires call that *exact* zone?

Almost none of us. Especially with young pitchers, a seventeen-inch-by-*two*-foot zone equals lotsa walks and boring baseball. Also, coaches and players—after all, it's *their* game—*still* don't like it. Any strike called much above the belt ("Johnny, never swing at anything above your hands!") draws such a beef, as does any ball called just under the knees ("Blue, my pitcher *lives* down there!") or close on the sides ("Blue, you gotta give 'im dat!") that the *de facto* strike zone is from around the navel to a bit below the knees and from about one ball-width inside the plate to about two outside (so seventeen inches wide becomes just over two feet).

Some umpires junk *any* formal zone, calling any pitch that can be hit decently a strike. This isn't as crazy as it sounds; after all, which came first, the strike zone or the plate? The strike zone evolved based on what could be hit and *then* was codified into a rule (no, Virginia, nobody named Doubleday sat down in 1839 and invented the game of "baseball" from scratch). Indeed, the first formal rules—published in 1858—defined a strike as a pitch "with in [sic] the legitimate reach of the bat." 'Nuther words, as I said in Q&A 1, hittable.

Most coaches say they don't care what we call as long as it's consistent. I like that, but I will add even consistency is tough to judge from stands, coaching boxes, and dugouts.

3. Why so much controversy over balls and strikes?

Several reasons: see Q&A 2; there are *hundreds* of pitches per game; pitchers aim for corners; no one else except the catcher has the close behind-the-plate perspective. I truly believe there are far fewer really bad calls than you think.

Consider:

1) People are naturally prejudiced toward their team. As one manual says, the plate umpire is "the only person in the park whose sole concern at that moment is whether the pitch is a ball or a strike." Can you show me another? Even one? No, everyone else either has an agenda or must be ready to react.

2) There's no wishful-thinking clause; if a pitcher who's been missing by miles misses close, you'll want it. Sorry; still a ball.

3) Where was I and where were you? Positioning is everything! I always want to chuckle when people dispute ball/strike calls from the dugout, the coaching box, or even the stands. I'm at arm's length, thinking of *nothing* else; they have *more* distance, a *worse* angle, *and* a favored team!

An umpire can *look* very consistent by playing off of the catcher: anything caught directly in front of the body or head without reaching or lunging or, on a pitch around the knees, turning the mitt over, looks like a strike from anywhere else.

That's not to say an umpire calling this way is actually *being* consistent. This is *not* about what the catcher can catch; it's about what the hitter can hit!

Speaking of catchers, one who keeps me from seeing the ball and/or the plate—whether by place, size, or movement— vastly reduces the chance of a strike call. This might not seem fair, but think objectively: if I can't see the baseball in the strike zone, how sure can I be it's a strike? (Remember, your answer goes both ways.)

4. What if only part of the ball is over the plate?

By rule, if any part of the ball touches any part of the strike zone, it's a strike.

5. What's this "natural stance" thing in the strike zone rule?

Now worded "as…prepared to swing," it aims to keep batters from shrinking the zone by crouching, but it can make the top of the zone *seem* to vary on different batters. In fact, if a batter's crouch varies, calls near the top of the zone may even *appear* to vary on different pitches to the same batter.

6. How could you call that a strike? I could see from here it was under the knees!

It's where the pitch passes the plate, *not* the batter—which is very tough to judge from the stands! It's hard for you even to *see* the plate from over there, not to mention that on a regulation field the batter can stand anywhere from two feet behind the point of the plate to four feet ahead of it!

7. How could you call that a strike? It bounced!

Great breaking pitches and not-so-great "rainbow" pitches! Have I ever called a pitch that bounced a strike and been sure I was right? Absolutely! (With all due respect to the professor who claims to have proved a pitch's change of direction is an optical illusion, I have *no* doubt breaking pitches actually break—and I'm sure most if not all batters agree!) Besides, on a regulation field a catcher might be as much as *eight feet* behind the point of the plate. So where did this bouncing pitch actually pass over it? This is also true *atop* the strike zone; that pitch caught directly behind the top of the batter's zone may well have been high as it passed over the plate.

8. How could you call that a strike? When it was halfway there, it was twice as high as my boy is tall!

A mother actually hollered this at me one day, after at *least* a ten-foot rainbow to her son. I'd *like* to have said, "Ma'am, I don't care if it came down with frost on it. It was over the plate within his vertical zone, and that's a strike!"

9. How could you call that a ball? The catcher never moved!

Is the catcher *directly* behind the plate? The catcher's box, which is rarely drawn, is almost *four* feet wide! A pitch to a catcher who's squatting a foot *off* the corner, quite legally, and doesn't move *does* look like a strike—over there in the stands! Not to me, behind the plate.

10. Why don't you tell the batter to go to first on ball four?

Many umpires do by saying "ball four" instead of "ball," but most of us believe players should have their heads in the game—and that starts with knowing how many balls and strikes you have. Especially when the next ball puts you on base!

11. What determines whether a ball is fair or foul?

This depends entirely on where the *ball*, not *any* part of the fielder, is. There are three ifs…

1) …on a ground ball that does *not* pass first or third, where it stops rolling or touches anything except the ground

2) …on a grounder that *does* pass either, where it does so

3) …on a fly ball that passes either base before it touches anything *including* the ground, where it does so (Exception: if it cleared the fence, it's where it did so and *not* where it landed—a critical call, because "fair" equals home run and "foul" usually equals strike, but so difficult from the inevitable distance that the big leagues first broke their antivideo replay policy for this play—and they routinely use *four* umpires, not two!)

The foul lines *should* be called fair lines: they are in fair ground. Yes, a batted ball that hits a *foul* line is a *fair* ball!

12. A batted ball hits home plate. Isn't it automatically foul?

No, and since the plate lies in fair territory, we umpires wonder how this myth started; if the plate were automatically anything, logic says it would be fair. Actually, the plate is considered part of the ground. That means a ball hitting it becomes fair or foul purely based on what follows per Q&A 11. However, the base bags—which are in fair territory—are not considered part of the ground; a batted ball that touches one is fair (even if it's because the bag's askew).

The pitcher's plate (usually called "the rubber") is also considered part of the ground, so a batted ball that ricochets off it into foul territory between home and first or third is foul, once stopped or touched. Impossible? It took twenty-five years, but I've actually seen that happen. Once.

13. Is a foul ball a strike, or isn't it?

About two-thirds of the time. Unless it would be the *third* strike, any uncaught foul except a *bunt* or a *foul tip* is a strike. There's no limit, either; theoretically, any at-bat could last for eternity; "four foul balls you're out" exists only in sandlots and a Statler Brothers song.

14. What's a bunt?

The batter uses the bat to block rather than hit the pitch, usually to advance a runner(s) while the defense gets the batter out—thus called a "sacrifice"—but also sometimes in hope of catching the defense off guard and beating the throw to first.

15. What's a foul tip?

Not *just* a swing and a nick; the ball must go "sharp and direct" to the catcher's hand or mitt *and* be caught. Exactly like a strike, this a live ball—baserunners *can* run. It *should* go without saying, but often doesn't, that if it's a third strike the batter is out. This rule was made to *help* batters; without it, as a batted ball caught on the fly, it would be a ridiculously cheap out. It also helps us umpires; this would be hotly disputed if that were the outcome.

However, if this is not *exactly* what happens, it's *not* a foul tip! If you say "foul tip," you've said, by definition, it was legally caught after first touching hand or mitt. No legal catch means *no* foul tip—just a foul ball. Since runners must return after uncaught fouls, coaches teach catchers to drop a tipped pitch if a stealing runner has a big jump. This is legal but risky, because the catcher can't *know* at the moment of this drop which way the umpire will rule.

16. Why call a player out just for taking off a helmet?

It's a safety rule, and we don't want to be sued. **The Runner(s)** being more likely to commit this, see Q&A 55.

17. How can you call the batter out for being out of the batter's box when there *isn't* any batter's box?

Nobody drew the boxes, huh?

First, what does the rule say? As the batter stands ready to hit, both feet must be completely inside the outside edges of the lines defining the box. There is no penalty; we simply tell and/ or show the batter where to be. Refusing to comply is refusing to get in the box—its own rule with its own penalty—but a rule now being tested in the minor leagues may change this (Q&A 75).

Now: a batter who hits the ball, fair or foul, while touching any ground outside and not touching the lines of the box is out.

18. But what if there *are* no lines?

If the batter's box isn't there, it's still there. Even if the lines were drawn—and they often aren't—they quickly get rubbed out as hitters dig in and take swings. I'll help a borderline batter by drawing a line in the dirt with the bat handle, but you just can't stop a game every few batters to re-chalk. The same people who say making this call without lines is unfair would complain just as bitterly, I have *no* doubt, if the *other* team's batter clearly stepped out of an undrawn box and hammered a home run. No doubt at all. We must, so to speak, draw the line somewhere!

However, we often make a tactical versus practical consideration in deciding where to draw it: after all, if the batter is a *smidgen* outside the box, especially if the box isn't visible, does it really make any difference? For me, it's two parts degree and one part intent. A good example is the hit-and-run play: one or more runners take off as the pitcher delivers, not actually trying to steal but to get a head start on a batted ball. In this play, the batter is to protect them from being thrown out by hitting the pitch no matter where it is—even if it's *not* hittable. Reaching and lunging are fine, but purposely stepping out of the box is breaking a rule to accomplish a mission rather than accidentally stepping slightly outside it while striding to generate bat speed. For me, that's a big difference in deciding whether to make this call.

19. Can the batter back out of the box at any time?

No, only when the ball is dead. Unless something else kills it, that means getting an umpire to call time. (Players do not call time; they *ask* for time. *Umpires* call time.) Once the pitcher has settled into the set position or started to wind up, time's a no-no; however, the umpire's reaction time after the batter's request can make the call *seem* late. In the real world, batters often leave the box without asking for time, and many umps then routinely grant it; how to enforce this is up to the umpire. If the batter backs out just as the pitcher starts to deliver and the ump doesn't grant time, though, a smart pitcher will complete the pitch. This is an automatic strike in high school; everywhere else it's called where pitched, but shouldn't the pitcher be able to hit the zone over an unguarded plate? (For a sidebar about **The Runner[s]**, see Q&A 50.)

20. Suppose the batter backs out *without* getting time and the pitcher starts to pitch then notices the batter's gone and stops. Is that a balk?

No, even though stopping in midpitch is the classic balk (Q&A 71). "Both…have violated a rule," as OBR words it, so they "start over from 'scratch.'"

21. So what if a batter *does* refuse to get into the box?

Now the batter *is* subject to automatic strikes; at any point, the umpire can stop telling the batter to get into the box and simply call a strike. This will be repeated until the batter relents or gets a third strike.

22. Why are there two batter's boxes?

Right-handed hitters bat from the one on, as seen from behind the plate, the left; left-handers from the one on the right. A "switch-hitter" can use either, obviously, but must decide *before* the pitcher gets in position to pitch; a switch can only be made when the pitcher isn't in position or the ball is dead.

23. What's this thing called the "Infield Fly Rule"?

Perhaps baseball's most misunderstood rule, this may be on your mind because of batter, runner, or fielder…or you're an Atlanta Braves fan. It was written to protect runners, so I'll answer this in **The Runner(s)**. Q&A 44. Have some time when you go there, though; the concept is simple, but the explanation is not.

24. What's interference?

Anything the offense (not just the batter; see Q&As 25 and 54) does that impedes the defense's play of the ball, resulting in an immediate dead ball and at least one out.

Here's something people *want* called "interference" that simply *isn't*: with a runner trying to steal third, a right-handed batter cannot *intentionally* hinder the catcher but does not have to disappear. (I know: "Stick it in his ear!" Well, whadaya want the batter to do? Dig a hole? Turn into a puff of smoke? Yell "incoming" and drop?)

In NCAA and FED, by the way, post-swing contact with the catcher or the ball—even accidental—is interference; OBR has an exception for this steal-swing-oops I call "half interference"—ball is dead, runners return, no one is out.

The defense can hinder the offense, but its illegal acts are called "obstruction (Q&A 86)." The only defensive infraction that's "interference" is hindering the batter's effort to hit a pitch, obviously almost always committed by the catcher (Q&A 31).

25. Can a batter be out for something someone else does?

Hey, it's a team game! Two examples: runner out on the front end of a double play interferes with the relay throw (Q&A 56); batter joins the walk to the dugout; teammate—including a base coach—physically or even verbally impedes a catch; batter is out.

26. Doesn't that extra line along the first-base line have something to do with interference?

Yes. Along and three feet from the latter half of that foul line, it defines "the three-foot lane" inside which a batter must run to first. Watch for this on bunts, choppers around the plate and uncaught third strikes. We only call this upon *actual* impediment—that is, the batter-runner is out of this lane and is either hit by the throw or causes it to be made badly or go uncaught.

27. Doesn't a batter who beats a throw to first base have to turn right after overrunning the bag?

Have to? No, but *should*. In this situation, a batter-runner who "attempts to run to second…is out when tagged." But what *is* an attempt? A lunge? A step? A lean? We can't read minds. Be safe; turn right! (Q&A 30)

28. What's a neighborhood call?

Nothing official, yet very much a part of the game. You'll hear the term after a groundout because it more directly involves **The Fielders;** I answer it in Q&A 83.

29. Isn't there a "one base on overthrow" rule?

How often have you heard that? Surprise! The answer is *no*! Why? This more directly affects **The Runner(s)**, so I answer in that section (Q&A 48).

30. Doesn't the plate umpire *have* to defer to a base umpire on a half swing?

Yes, *if* asked by the catcher or defensive manager *and* the call was "ball." (Seems overstated to me—why would the defense appeal a strike?—but that's the wording.)

See, if I'm working the plate and rule it a strike, I either saw the ball touch the strike zone or I saw the batter try to hit it. But my priority is the pitch location, so the rule concedes doubt on the swing and requires me to "get help." This, the only *mandatory* check by one umpire to another in all of baseball, actually *frees* the plate ump to concentrate on the pitch. Like any appeal (Q&A 59), it must be requested before the next pitch, play, or attempted play (FED: next pitch).

FED allows the plate umpire to decline, but I agree with OBR/NCAA. FED argues that a solo base umpire has no better angle—even, from the right-field line with a left-handed batter, a worse one. True, but the base ump isn't worried about pitch location. A base ump who can't tell can (should) just let the call stand; I believe it's well worth requiring the check.

Wondering what's a swing? On that, OBR is silent. NCAA defines it as the barrel of the bat passing the batter's front hip. I *agree* with that but would not *limit* it to that. You'll hear many other criteria: the batter "broke" or "rolled" the wrists; the bat passed the front plane of the plate; the bat was moving forward as it and ball passed each other. Manuals say we just have to judge "whether the batter actually struck at the ball."

Similarly, when bunting, nothing in OBR requires pulling the bat back to avoid a strike; the umpire simply decides whether the batter tried to make contact. Since bunting is an effort to block rather than hit the ball, though, some say holding the bat motionless in the path of the pitch can be an attempt. (FED specifies no strike on this, but since umpires argue it strenuously

THE "KILL THE UMPIRE" HANDBOOK

both ways, it's fair to say there's room for argument.) So, like turning right at first (Q&A 27), pulling the bat back is the *smart* thing to do. Some rules may imply we can read minds, but we really can't; try to make such things obvious!

31. Why does the batter get first base if the bat just nicks the catcher's mitt?

The mitt impeded the bat, therefore the offense. Look, a difference of a fraction of an inch when bat meets ball may make one of feet when ball meets turf. What would have happened if the bat hadn't "just nicked" the mitt?

32. Why is this call often controversial?

"Just nicks" seems like such a little thing; you may not even be able to hear it in the stands. Also, with wood bats, it's easily mistaken for a foul tip (Q&A 15). The standard "too deep in the box" argument holds no water if the umpire is paying attention to the batter's feet (Q&As 17 and 18); if not, well, the ump should be—but this is simply not correctible. (I'm gonna ask the base ump, five times as far away, where the batter's feet were relative to an often rubbed-out line?) If the rear foot was legal, unless the clip of the mitt was on purpose (batter's interference; if flagrant, worthy of ejection), the catcher was just too close.

It's also one of a few calls that are sometimes, by rule, ignored. I once had two in the same game, and up in the stands, the coach's wife really sold me down the river for "calling" it one time and not the other. In fact, I signaled delayed dead ball

21

(Q&A 90) both times; but on one, the batter reached base, all runners advanced, and no one was out. By rule, play proceeds as if there'd been no violation—something a coach's wife ought to know! There is a third possibility: if the batter gets on but any runner either doesn't advance or is put out, the offense chooses between play and penalty.

33. **Can the batter always try for first base when the catcher doesn't catch a third strike?**

Not always. This rule confuses for a couple of reasons.

First, many leagues for players twelve and under don't use it. This can confuse spectators who know the rule but don't know the game they're watching doesn't have it. (I suppose it also confuses some parents of thirteen-year-olds—for a while.)

Second, there's an exception that fans, players, and even coaches forget in that adrenaline-charged moment that the ball rolls loose. Everyone yells at the batter to run—but was there a runner at first? If so, how many out?

The batter is *not* immediately out on an *uncaught* third strike *unless* first base is occupied with less than two out. It's easier to grasp this confusing "unless" if you know *why* it exists: so a strikeout can't start a force double play (Q&A 43). With first base empty, there's no force, so no force double play is possible; with two out, of course, no double play of any kind is possible. The trouble is, fans yell for the batter to run, who does, and then other runners run because they *think* they're forced.

There *is* no force—there never was—but any runner trapped off base this way and tagged *is* out. The umpire should not have to think about this; we thought about it when the count *got* to two strikes. That's one of the differences between umpiring and paid spectating.

34. What if a batter who *can* run doesn't? Isn't that an out?

Yes, but not immediately. Either the batter or first base must be legally tagged or—if not—the batter is out upon leaving the plate area. That's a recent rule change—used to be upon getting to the dugout—but many umpires have always called it this way.

You'll hear of "abandoning the effort to advance," but that rule doesn't apply until a batter-runner reaches first base.

35. Doesn't the catcher have to *drop* the ball on this play?

Not necessarily; once any pitch bounces, even if then caught cleanly, it is not a legal catch. Because it's *usually* triggered by the catcher dropping a pitch, fans call this the "dropped third strike" rule, but umpires use the terminology I've already written here twice: the "*uncaught* third strike" rule. It's a wording thing: the definition of "catch" includes the phrase "in flight," so a pitch that was not caught in the air was not *legally* caught.

36. Any *other* quirks about this rule?

With the bases loaded and two out, if a third strike is not legally caught but recovered quickly enough, the fielder with the ball can end the inning simply by stepping on the plate. Why?

By definition, this *is* a force play (Q&A 43) on the runner from third, but that's easy to forget when a force starts without a *batted* ball.

37. Doesn't a batter hit by a pitch *always* get first base?

Almost always. (The official term—"touches"—is quite literal, even if it just grazes the batter's clothing. That's why we might tell a batter to tuck in a shirt or stuff a dangling batting glove down inside a pants pocket.) I say *almost* because if the batter…

1) …doesn't try to get out of the way, assuming the "touch" isn't in the strike zone, it's just a ball—something to remember when your kid's teammates are yelling "Take one for the team!"

2) …*is* touched in the strike zone, regardless of trying to get out of the way, it's a strike.

3) …is trying to hit the pitch when touched, it's also a strike—and as outlandish as that sounds, I've seen it happen.

A pitched ball that touches a batter is *always* instantly dead.

38. Say a pitch bounces and then hits the batter. First base?

Sure. I see your logic: a pitch that bounces through the strike zone is a ball. But that pitch isn't dead; it's just not, by definition, a strike. Still a live pitch, it can even be batted and fielded—and any live pitch that touches a batter awards first base except as noted in Q&A 37.

39. What if the batter and the throw get to first base at *exactly* the same time?

Spend much time around baseball and you'll hear "The tie goes to the runner!" I've heard it stated as fact *and* derided as myth. While there's no such wording in OBR, this is a *practical* fact: "a batter is out when...after hitting a fair ball, the batter-runner or first base is tagged *before* said batter-runner reaches first base." Before? Aha! A tie *would* draw a safe call—but in over forty years, I never saw a tie. (Q&A 65)

40. What happens when the wrong batter is at the plate?

This rule takes almost *two* pages of OBR, but it's pretty simple.

If the offense realizes the mistake *during* the at-bat, the proper batter replaces the improper one and assumes the count of balls and strikes. Otherwise, nothing happens unless the defense appeals, and a smart manager waits for the right moment. Why? Say an improper batter makes an out. Great, says the defense. Instead, say there's a hit. Now the defense appeals! Hit...what hit? It's an out! And it nullifies runner advances made because of the at-bat; advances made *without* the batter's work—steals, balks, throwaways and pitches that get past the catcher—stand.

However, if a wrong batter completes a turn at bat and a pitch is thrown to the next batter, that next batter *becomes* the proper batter and play goes on. Sorry, but there's a "however" to *that* "however"—it applies only to that time at bat. If, say, an errant copy of a lineup card has this happening every turn through the order, the defense can appeal it after any turn—or not at all.

Such a chain of events can end up with the batter who should be up already on base, in which case the next batter in the order becomes the proper batter.

Did I say this was simple?

41. Why doesn't the umpire replace a wrong batter?

It's up to the batting team to keep itself straight. No official—including a stadium announcer—should let on when the wrong batter's up, so the defense can make the most it can of its opponents' mistake (Q&A 40).

II. The Runner(s)

42. What's the difference between tagging and tagging up?

Both involve touching.

A fielder touches a runner or a base to get an out while a runner tags up by touching a base in the hope of advancing to another base. A fielder can tag a runner with ball in hand or glove, but can tag a base by touching it with any part of the body while holding the ball.

Runner(s) may tag up after a fly ball is caught, unless the catch ends the inning. Any runner off base at the catch (by definition, in the air) must touch that base before a fielder tags it or the runner. After touching the base, the runner may try to advance.

The rules specifically say runners may leave the bag when the fielder first touches—not actually "catches"—the ball. How unfair would it be for a runner to be out for leaving before the catch if that was only because the fielder juggled the ball? (And how soon would fielders start doing it on purpose?)

43. What's a force play?

Only one runner may occupy a base. Therefore, when the batter becomes a runner, all runners without an empty base behind them are "forced" to the next base. Any runner tagged while off base is out, but so is any forced runner when *the next base* is tagged.

This—a "force-out"—allows baseball's most exciting events, the double play and extremely rare triple play (yeah, I like 'em better than homers—flow and precision over brute strength, I guess). However, it also forced—pardon the pun—baseball to create its least understood rule, the "Infield Fly Rule" (Q&A 44).

44. Yeah, what's this thing called the "Infield Fly Rule"?

This is easier to understand if you know its *why*: to resolve an unintended conflict between two other rules. Runners are *sometimes* forced to try for the next base (Q&A 43), but *any* runner can be put out for not tagging up after a caught fly (Q&A 42). So, some sly and wily infielder in the misty days of bygone-ball—this rule was added in 1895—figured out how to get two outs from one pop-up: await the ball and play per the runners. They go? Catch the ball in the air for one out and throw to a vacated base for another. They don't? Let it land, pick it up, and make whatever throw best starts a double or even triple play; no matter what the offense does, at least two runners will be out. This was so unfair that the rules chefs cooked up the following: *when there are at least two forced runners and an umpire decides*

*that a pop fly "can be caught by an infielder with ordinary effort,"
an infield fly is declared. The batter is immediately out, removing
the force play.*

If this ball lands foul—or fair, untouched, and then becomes
foul (Q&A 11)—the foul supersedes the infield fly.

Why require more than one force? The batter can get to
first on a pop fly, so this won't get two outs with only a runner
on first.

Let's try to reinforce away all confusion over this rule:

1) It requires at least two forced runners at the time of the
   pitch; OBR words it "at first and second *or* first, second,
   and third," but it's *this* simple: *if there's a forced runner at
   second base*. If so, there must also be a runner at first—
   and that makes two, right?

2) The ball remains alive.

3) It applies *only* to full-swing pop flies, *not* bunts or line
   drives.

4) The ball ending up foul simply erases the call. Nothing
   complicated about that: the ball is dead, and everybody
   simply resets.

5) Runners *may* run but, like any fly, if the ball is legally
   caught in the air a tag of such a runner or of the vacated
   base is an out.

6) If the ball is not caught, regardless what the runners do, the batter is *still* out and therefore there is still no force. (Would you believe I've had this argued? It's the *point*!) This does, though, nullify the need to tag up (Q&A 42)—an incentive for the defense to catch it despite the already-called out.

7) A fly ball into the outfield *can* be an infield fly; a shortstop drifting into left field is still an infielder, and *how* far matters not to whether it's "ordinary effort." (P.S.: I wrote that more than fifteen *years* before the infamous Atlanta pop-up of October 5, 2012.)

At the risk of *adding* to confusion, a separate rule says that with *any* forced runners—even one—no infielder may intentionally drop a fly ball—*even* a bunt or line drive. If that happens, the batter is out, the ball is dead, and all runners return. Different rule, similar intent; starting a double play is the only reason a fielder would do this. (A pitcher once *swore* to me, after using both hands to guide a soft line drive to the turf and then snatching it up, "I didn't *either* drop that on purpose!" I said, "So you object to a 'bad' call that *gave* you an out?" He stalked back to the mound, muttering something I chose not to hear.)

45. Riddle me this: when is a force not a force?

When it's been removed by a previous out. Classic example: runner on first, batter hits grounder there, runner takes off, fielder tags first *before* throwing to second—there's now no force. (The well-coached first baseman shouts "Tag!" while throwing.)

46. What happens when there's more than one runner on the same base?

Best advice I ever heard: "Tag everybody and let the umpires sort it out!" That's actually very practical! Here's the sort-out: the *following* runner is out *when tagged*. Absent a force, the *lead* runner has the right to the base, but there's no *automatic* out. Even if there are *three* on a base, *nobody* is out until somebody— the *right* somebody, at that—is tagged.

Such a play started my writing this. I'm in the stands when a play had runners looking like Keystone Kops, and the ball was thrown all over the lot. When two boys ended up on third, the third-base coach sent the trailing one back. After he made it, some guy pontificated, "That second runner shoulda been called out while they were both touching third." Calm and articulate, he sounded right even though he wasn't. Despite being correct, my colleague was roundly booed. (Bud, this book's for you.)

47. If one of these runners tried to go back, wouldn't that be an out for running the bases backward?

That applies only if the runner has "legal possession of a base"—here, the second runner doesn't—*and* if it is "for the purpose of confusing the defense or making a travesty of the game." Great phrase; doesn't describe retreating from a bag full of teammate.

PATRICK M. SULLIVAN

I have invoked this, though. With runners on first and third but not second, the runner from first may take off as if to steal and then slow down or even stop; the idea is to draw a throw to second and let the teammate score from third. That's legal, but let the runner touch second and then retreat and all necessary elements are there for an out to be called.

48. Isn't there a "one base on overthrow" rule?

Only in backyards and sandlots. Rules granting free bases are confusing because they're many, they're detailed, and they're rarely used. The issue isn't really the ball going "over" its target, though; it's going into dead-ball territory.

Everybody knows everybody gets home when a fair ball leaves the playing field (provided the fence is far enough away; the minimums vary by level). Now, what if a fielder intentionally touches a fair ball with something not intended for that—say, a cap—or throws a glove at and hits a fair ball? Three bases! What if this is at a thrown rather than batted ball? Two bases! What's more, the defense had better get after it; in all of those cases, the ball remains alive so the runner(s) can go for more!

Everybody also knows a fair ball that bounces over the fence (again, really because the ball is dead) awards two bases from offensive players' positions at the pitch, the proverbial (although a misnomer) ground-rule double. What if a *throw* goes into the stands? Also two bases, but from where? If it was by an infielder making the *first* play on the batted ball, from where the run-

32

ners were at the pitch; otherwise, from where they were when the throw was released. Some coaches call the latter "one-plus-one"—next base plus one more. The rule has no such wording, but as a practical matter, this coaching catch-phrase is accurate.

The only rule that actually awards one base after an overthrow (again, really a throw that becomes dead) covers the pitcher throwing the ball away while trying to pick off a runner. However, this rule applies only while on the rubber. So if the pitcher "clearly and distinctly" steps off it before throwing the ball away, the award is two bases.

49. What if a pitched ball goes through the backstop?

If a pitch becomes dead in *any* way that does not involve touching bat or batter, all runners get one base. (Does the batter? Only if it happens to be ball four or an uncaught third strike [Q&A 33].) This includes going through the backstop, *or* sticking in it *or* in the "catcher or umpire's mask or paraphernalia." For years, I thought that last one could only happen to umpires who use the outside chest protector—until it happened to me while I was wearing my inside one: a pitch sailed between the catcher's legs and my legs, then ricocheted off the backstop into my ball bag! Both coaches were stunned to learn a rule covered this, which I think demonstrates just how thorough our rules are! (Since writing this, I've seen a video of a wild pitch disappearing, until the plate ump finds it *in his shirt pocket*!)

50. Can a runner be picked off when the batter is not in the batter's box?

I've had many lively discussions grounded in, "The ball can't be alive if the batter isn't in the box!" Here's why that's not true:

OBR only once says a batter must be in the box for the ball to be made live, and that is specific to starting the game. Otherwise, defining live and dead balls, the rules say "after the umpire calls 'Play' the ball is alive and in play and remains alive and in play until, for legal cause, or at the umpire's call of 'Time' suspending play, the ball becomes dead." Therefore, if a batter backs out without getting time, the ball remains alive (Q&A 19). What's more, the batter does not have to be in the box for a dead ball to be made live: OBR says the "plate umpire *shall* call 'Play' *as soon as* the pitcher takes position on his plate with the ball in his possession." The italics are mine, to stress the fact that, technically, awaiting the batter isn't even an option. Many umps do wait to avoid making the pitcher think we're calling for a pitch; this is not a good idea if the batter isn't set in the box. Others don't signal a live ball at all because the rule so explicitly makes it live when the pitcher takes position.

So no, it is not even *unusual* to have a live ball with no batter in the box, and any runner tagged with any live ball is out!

51. Stealing home can lead to some hairy situations, can't it?

Yes, and not just the obvious one of beating the ball and getting beaned. The catcher's instinct will be to leap forward, catch the pitch, and tag the runner, but doing so can't preempt the batter's chance to hit. If the mitt goes over the plate, the ump should kill the play and award a base to everyone (including that runner stealing home, scoring a run). This kind of catcher's interference (Q&A 24) is technically a balk, even though the pitcher didn't do it. It is, I believe, the single toughest infield call in the game. Just look at everything the umpire must see, follow, and evaluate!

52. What if the runner *does* beat the pitch there and get beaned?

The ball's dead, but the play stands. The runner, assuming the plate is touched, is safe, and the pitch counts as called. The run counts *unless* the pitch was a third strike for a third out; in that case, the inning's end precedes and therefore prevents the run.

53. Don't runners have to stay in the baseline?

Yes, but two things about this rule mess people up. First, the baseline is not the line between the bases; that's the base *path*. The *baseline* is a line from where the runner is to the base being sought. Second, it applies only *when trying to avoid being tagged*. It limits runners to three feet (since we don't carry yardsticks, we interpret this as a full step) from this direct line. Now, the runner doesn't *always* own this path; any fielder playing a thrown or batted ball must be avoided, *even* if in the baseline.

54. What's interference?

Any act that impedes the defense's play of a batted ball (see Q&As 24 and 86). Technically, this includes purposely getting into, or hesitating in, the line of vision of a player trying to field a ball, but that one is enforced less than I'd like. I know it borders on mindreading, but why else does a guy who can run like a March wind move like molasses in January?

55. Why call a player out just for taking off a helmet?

Because I don't want the player hurt or me sued. I'm the first person *you*, the parent of an injured player, will look to sue. (Some leagues penalize this with an ejection instead of or in addition to an out.) Offensive players *must* keep their helmets on while the ball is live, even if the play seems over. One snap throw and an inattentive player can get hit in the head. Youth leagues also strictly enforce helmets on catchers warming up pitchers, both before the inning and in the bullpen. Most umpires will issue a warning, but remember: these rules are for *your* youngster's safety. An out or ejection will be remembered a lot longer than a warning.

56. Can a runner be called out because of something someone else does?

That's true of a force out (see Q&A 43), caused by the batter, but I assume you're asking in the context of rules violations:

1) Runner tries to steal home; batter interferes with catcher; runner is out (unless there are already two out, be-

cause that will almost always bring up a weaker batter leading off the next inning).

2) Baserunner makes time-honored effort to "break up the double play" and does something the umpire sees as interference: batter joins runner in the jog back to the dugout (Q&A 25).

3) Base coach interferes with play: somebody's out. This usually involves getting in the way of an infielder trying to catch a foul pop fly or retrieve an errant throw, but it can be more direct. Say a runner ignores a stop sign and is stopped by a third-base coach's physical *grab*. Stopped? That runner's *out*!

57. What if a batted ball hits a runner?

If the contact is in foul territory, where smart runners lead off third base, just a bruise and a foul ball. (Well, maybe not a "bruise"; the rule says "touches.") In fair ground, this is *usually* an out. What else? The ball is dead, the batter gets first base and credit for a hit, and all unforced runners return to the base they held at the pitch. If a batted ball hits *an umpire* in fair ground, the result is the same. Oh, except the umpire is *not* out.

I say "usually"—if the ball first passes an infielder other than the pitcher, by rule, we ignore it because the defense had a fair shot. Also, a fair fly that deflects off a fielder into a runner or umpire and is caught in the air is *not a catch*, but it is alive, so the fielder can throw for an out just as if it were a ground ball.

58. Since bases are the runner's sanctuaries, is a runner who's hit by a batted ball while on a base safe?

Nicely loaded question, but *unless* this was a declared Infield Fly (Q&A 44), the runner is out. The "unless" addresses the fact that a runner in this situation simply has nowhere safe to go; "declared" is an odd word because an infield fly can be declared retroactively.

59. What happens when a runner misses a base or leaves too soon when tagging up?

Most of the time, way too much happens.

In what is called an appeal, a fielder tells an umpire a runner either missed a bag or left it too soon and tags one or the other. Unless the ball is dead (no one can be put out with a dead ball), that's all we need. Notice that umpires do *not* initiate these.

However, many coaches *always* have their pitcher take the ball to the mound, assume a ready-to-pitch position, step off, state which runner did what at which base, throw to a fielder on that base, and look at us for an out call; they seem to think either the procedure at the mound is part of the appeal process or the pitcher has to do the talking. Actually, *any* fielder can voice an appeal and the procedure on the mound is only necessary if the ball is dead—that's how to make a dead ball live (Q&A 50).

The appeal must precede the next pitch, play, or attempted play (except FED: next pitch)—or after a third out, "before the defensive team leaves the field," i.e., when the pitcher and all infielders are off fair territory. (Yes, the inning's over, but you'll want to appeal if it negates a run or brings up a weaker batter first next inning.) Doing it with a live ball doesn't kill the appeal by rule, but if the pitcher steps off incorrectly it's a balk and a balk is a "play" so that *would* kill it (except in FED; same rules difference). If the ball is alive—as it is unless it went out of play or an umpire called time—the appeal *should* be made immediately.

60. So all that's needed is to tag the missed bag, or the runner who missed it, with a live ball?

Nope, the defense must "unmistakably" appeal to the ump. What does *that* mean? Well, OBR specifically states that "a player, inadvertently stepping on the base with a ball in hand, would not constitute an appeal."

61. Then why have I seen umps ring up a runner for this without any tag?

You've been watching high school games! After FED dropped appeals decades ago, umpires called runners out, without appeal, when no further play was possible or the ball became dead. (Calling it with play in progress could cause confusion, like whether there is or isn't a force.) The idea was to speed things up, but in my experience, it backfired. The very act of the appeal shows the umpire wasn't the only one seeing something; lacking that, this time-saving change ramped up time-wasting arguments.

Note my past tense, though; FED now has a "modified" appeal. Upon a simple verbal appeal, the ump rules—still, immediately if the ball's dead but, if it's alive, when no further play is possible. This is much better because it demonstrates somebody besides the umpire saw something.

62. What's the rule on leaving base early in no-leadoff leagues?

First, it exists only in younger levels—as far as I know, nowhere for boys over twelve. Second, the particulars vary. Usually, after pitcher and catcher are in position, no runner may break contact with the bag until the pitch reaches the plate, batter or catcher—all within an eyelash of the same thing, of course, it's just whichever way the organization chooses to state it. Some leagues, with base distances that are longer than Little League® but shorter than OBR, let the runners leave when the pitcher releases the ball, like in fast-pitch softball.)

At least two youth organizations' rules call for umpires to throw a flag (or their hat, which I think looks absolutely ridiculous) when a runner leaves a base too soon. A flag is a wonderful idea because it no longer looks as if we reversed a play, and the sand-weighted flags used in football are ideal. Little League® rule books did reference flags when I was umpiring there, but nobody used them and I wasn't going to be the only one. However, from what I see in online umpiring forums, the idea has since caught on.

The penalty varies. In some leagues, offending runners are out; in others, they simply return to the base, unless thrown out, in which case the violation is ignored. It's simple—unless the batter hits that pitch into fair territory...

A violation by *any* runner affects *all* runners. On a multiple steal, for example, all runners must return even though one leaving early doesn't help another steal. What's more, on a fair ball that results in no outs, all runners may go only as far as forced by the batter's progress. This can get hairy: runner on second, only; leaves early; batter doubles. The runner, who has surely scored, must return to third. This may not seem fair, but remember the point: don't leave early!

A plate umpire once overruled me on this very play in a Little League® tournament game, but he was wrong—*twice*. Not only did he get the rule wrong, scoring the culprit I'd put on third, he had no right to change or even question my call unless I asked for his opinion (Q&A 96)—even if the offense complained, which I didn't see but assume must have happened, and I would have consulted him if that had been the case. (Yes, the plate umpire is in charge, but that authority has limits. They're called "rules.") I didn't think it wise to make an issue of this without input from the wronged team, who did not protest. This was an early round of the tournament that leads to the Little League® World Series, and I could see a disagreement *between* umpires going all the way to Williamsport and maybe making news. No, thanks. For once in my life, I exercised the better part of valor.

Now, I have a question for *you*: with the bases loaded, a runner leaves early and the batter reaches first on a ball hit within the infield. What do you do? There's no "back" to send them to!

Some no-leadoff leagues have a special rule: the runner from third goes to the dugout with neither run scored nor out recorded while the advances by the other runners and the batter stand; that is, the runner on third is erased. Umpires call this the "poof play" because the runner vanishes! It's *seriously* counter to the spirit of the game, but if you play without leadoffs, you're going to have to do some compromising. Here, the only other options condone this infraction by allowing a run or charge an out for a violation that doesn't warrant one.

This do-over lets the batter, standing on first base, keep the successful at-bat rather than go back and maybe make an out.

63. Suppose a runner leaves early but goes back, whether to correct the mistake or tag up after a fly. Does the penalty still apply?

Sorry, any runner who leaves early irreversibly affects that pitch and any resulting play. (For "tagging up," see Q&A 42.)

64. If a batter is called out for batting out of order and a runner advanced during the at-bat, does the runner have to go back?

If the advance had nothing to do with the batter—steal, balk, pitch getting past the catcher—the runner stays. If the advance was because of any action by that batter, even an out, it's back to the previous bag. (Q&A 40)

65. On a force, what if the throw and the runner get there at *exactly* the same time?

Like Q&A 39, the tie goes to the runner—on any non-tag play, not just a force!

66. Isn't tagging the runner *always* required on a non-force play?

Nope. Neither a runner who's off base when a fly ball is caught nor one returning to a missed base is, by definition, forced, but in both cases either the runner or the appropriate base can be tagged for an out. (Q&A 59)

67. What do you mean, out? Never got touched!

Let's talk about tagging runners in **The Fielders** (Q&A 81).

68. What's a neighborhood call?

Often invoked about calls on the front end of a double play, this benefits **The Fielders** and is answered in Q&A 83.

69. What's a balk?

A free pass to the next base for all baserunners, but not the batter. Other than that, it's a simple question with a very complicated answer. Since balks are almost always committed by the pitcher, you'll find the answer(s) in that section (Q&A 71).

III. The Pitcher

70. What's the strike zone?

See Q&A 1, but it isn't as simple as you think. That's why the next *eight* questions also deal with ball/strike calls.

71. What's a balk?

There are more than a dozen answers in the actual balk rule, with several others scattered elsewhere through the rules. The many ways and their detail complicate it, but the concept is simple: a pitcher can't try to fool a batter or runner by starting to pitch and then throwing to a base, or vice versa, or by starting but not finishing a pitch.

One thing that should be obvious, but apparently isn't: it is *impossible* to balk with a dead ball. Less obviously: most balk possibilities go away when the pitcher legally leaves the rubber (technically, the pitcher's plate).

Verbiage and variety are two reasons this rule confuses; another, frankly, is inconsistent enforcement. This starts with

"If we called every balk we saw, we'd never get the game played!" Also, different leagues want different things called, sometimes changing even within the season. ("Go easy early, but tighten up in time to get them ready for the tournaments.") Deceiving batter or runner being the reason for most balk rules, we also try to consider whether the pitcher is *trying* to deceive or just doesn't know any better—but reading minds is not a science.

Balks called without the intent test primarily protect the batter: stopping in mid-pitch, unless the batter first backed out of the box; making any motion that looks as if you're pitching when you're not; when on the rubber, dropping the ball (unless there are no runners, in which case this is a ball in the count if it rolls across the foul line and nothing if it doesn't); once in either ready-to-pitch stance, separating the hands except in the act of pitching. That particular balk, however, is "not applicable in Little League®" under its modifications to OBR.

The foot the pitcher plants is the "pivot" foot; the other is the "free" foot. So from the windup, if the foot on the glove side of the body moves, a pitch must follow; or from the set, either a pitch or a step-and-throw to an occupied base. Any other move off the rubber *must* start with the pivot foot. *Anything* else is a balk.

In games with leadoffs, you may see a pitcher get into the windup stance as if forgetting there's a runner, then suddenly step back with the pivot foot and try to pick one off. Deceptive? Yes, but by rule perfectly legal.

Most balks that protect runners only matter in games with leadoffs: from the rubber, throwing to a base without first stepping toward it; stepping off the rubber with the free foot, or toward the plate or first base with either foot. One that matters *even* in no-leadoff games is standing without the ball "on or astride" (all FED games have leadoffs, but its rule is within five feet of) the rubber; it sells runners the falsehood that the pitcher has the ball when a fielder does, setting up the "hidden ball trick."

Some balks are grayer in all levels: taking the catcher's sign while not touching the rubber (intended to prevent quick-pitching but so tough for a two-person crew to enforce that we simply enforce the quick-pitch rule [Q&A 78]); when using the set position, not stopping before pitching (but that old argument over what constitutes a stop [one second? discernible? change of direction?] will still be going on when Ken Griffey's grandson gets to the Majors. Honestly, this rule is clearer than its lack of enforcement suggests, but no umpire can be the only one calling any certain kind of balk).

Technically, pitchers can't fake to first or third base. Practically, they can, if they first step back off the rubber with the pivot foot. Until recently, they *could* fake to third from the rubber, which allowed another tricky but legal move. With runners on at least first and third, a right-handed pitcher would fake to third then wheel toward first. Assuming the rubber was disengaged in the process, a subsequent fake to first was legal.

Controversy often ensued—"Did the pitcher *actually* leave the rubber?"—and finally OBR simply banned the fake to third. We'll see if FED and/or NCAA follow suit.

Actions by the pitcher's teammates can result in a balk. Say the catcher is outside the catcher's box when the pitch is released; during an intentional walk, anticipation makes it easy to set up outside it or jump out too soon (this is very technical, of little real impact, based on lines even less likely than the batter's box to be visible, and so rarely enforced). Say the pitcher delivers while any fielder except the catcher is in foul ground; this usually involves a first baseman outside the foul line while holding a runner, or a leftfielder sneaking in behind a runner on third. A third way can be found in Q&A 51.

Turning the shoulder while checking a runner at first base is a balk in some games and not in others. That's because OBR and NCAA trigger pitching regulations when the pitcher assumes a legal pre-pitch stance, but FED does when the pitcher intentionally touches the rubber. Also, in most of baseball a balk is a *delayed* dead ball; so if the pitcher balks and then throws the ball away trying to pick off a runner or pitches into a play in which all offensive players advance with no one put out, we ignore the balk in favor of the play. In FED, though, the balk is an *immediate dead ball*. (Don't ask me why.) Imagine you're at the plate... The pitcher balks but pitches...You hit it out... Noooo—your circuit clout doesn't count...

72. **If a pitcher balks and pitches and the batter does not hit it, does the pitch count toward balls and strikes?**

Never in FED; the balk killed the ball *before* the pitch. It *can* in OBR and NCAA, more as a side effect than a rule difference. Because those ignore a balk if everybody advances with no outs *and* if the un-hit pitch puts the batter on base—ball four, or the ways in Q&As 31, 33, and 37—the pitch counts (but of course, that ends the at-bat). Otherwise, the balk stands with all runners moving up one base and the batter returning to the plate with the count of balls and strikes that existed before the balk.

73. **Isn't throwing to an empty base a balk?**

Even *faking* to an unoccupied base is a balk; once the batter is in position, so is throwing to anyone but the catcher or an occupied base. However, both rules have contexts offensive coaches can't seem to remember: one contains the phrase "except for the purpose of making a play"—trying to retire a runner certainly qualifies—and the other applies only if the pitcher does this in order to "intentionally delay the game."

Offensive coaches want this, say, when a pitcher throws to the shortstop in position rather than at second base as a runner leads off. This runner is often closer to the fielder than the bag, though, so as far as I'm concerned that is an attempt at "making a play" and is not just to "delay the game." To disagree, you gotta believe the shortstop won't even try to tag the runner!

74. How many times can a coach go to the mound before the pitcher has to leave the game?

OBR says the second visit in the same inning; in FED, it's the fourth in the game plus one per any extra inning; NCAA incorporates both. Youth leagues often inflate this rule, then ask us to ignore it. ("This is instructional baseball; let us teach and let them learn.") Many youth leagues also limit how long a pitcher may pitch, either by number of pitches or number of innings (if the latter, a single pitch in an inning counts as an inning).

By the way, about that phrase "to the mound"—meetings in Little League® games happen at the foul line rather than on the mound because its coaches are not allowed to cross that line. The stated idea is to keep the spotlight on the players.

75. Speaking of limits, isn't there a time limit on the pitcher?

It's about time—literally. Once the pitcher has the ball and the batter is ready, unless there are runners, OBR requires a pitch within twelve seconds on penalty of a ball being added to the count. The limit was twenty seconds when the rule was adopted in 1957, as it still is in NCAA and FED, and umpires actually used stopwatches back then. FED's rule applies even with runners, but a pickoff try as well as a pitch resets the clock.

There are similar efforts to save time with batters. FED gives the batter twenty seconds to get into the box, NCAA fifteen. A rule that started in FED and has filtered up requires batters to keep at least one foot in the box between pitches, on penalty of a strike. Multiple exceptions mean the batter can still leave the box more often than not, but it's a "step" in the right direction. Still, in the years since it was added, I've neither called it nor seen it called; its value is in the reminder, or rather its threat.

Some minor leagues are testing on-field clocks. The official pro rule is still twelve seconds from when both pitcher and batter are ready, but these clocks count down from twenty starting from when the pitcher receives the ball. A pitch, pick-off try, or umpire's whim resets them, but if the batter isn't ready to hit when the countdown clock gets to :05, a strike is called; and if the pitcher doesn't either begin the pitching motion or try a pickoff by :00, it's a ball. This experiment is at the behest of Major League Baseball, which means you'll likely see some form of this there eventually. The clock also counts down to the scheduled start time and ticks off 2:25 between half innings.

76. And what's the limit on warm-up pitches?

OBR allows eight "preparatory" pitches but also says they "shall not consume more than one minute." FED agrees for a pitcher's first inning but cuts it to five for returning hurlers. Here, NCAA sides with FED; however, many umps use 8/5 everywhere, and no one seems to object. Technically, this warm-up time starts the moment the previous half inning ends, but I'll allow thirty seconds or so for the pitcher and catcher to get out there. If they dally beyond that or no one takes the warm-ups for a catcher who isn't ready, I can and will give a pitcher less time.

Because the reliever didn't get to warm up in the bullpen, a replacement for an *injured* pitcher gets all the time and/or pitches the umpire (not the reliever, contrary to broadcasters everywhere) deems necessary. However, because the rule refers to a pitcher being "summoned into the game" it does not provide extra throws to a reliever who was playing another position and so didn't get to warm up.

77. Why do some umps make my kid change gloves to pitch?

The pitcher is more regulated than any other player on the field, and not just by balks (Q&A 71) and time limits (Q&A 75). The glove can't be white or gray and must be a single color (I've never seen the latter enforced) nor are sweat bands on the arms or wrists or a batting glove under the mitt legal. These rules exist to avoid distracting the batter, which is also why we might make a pitcher tuck in a batting glove hanging from the pocket or lose an under-shirt with floppy sleeves.

As regulated as the pitcher is, there is a right no one else has: asking for a different baseball without stating any reason.

78. What's an illegal pitch?

Most notably: pitching a doctored baseball (called a "spit ball" in the rules because it was originally done with saliva). This applies to anything from applying any "foreign substance" to scuffing or even cutting the baseball intentionally) and quick-pitching (pitching when the batter isn't ready; note I didn't just say "in the box" but "ready"). The penalty for a quick pitch is a balk if there are runners and a ball if there are not; the penalty for doctoring is ejection.

79. Speaking of spitballs, isn't there a rule about pitchers' touching their mouths?

Yes, but most youth pitchers can't throw a spitball effectively, so many youth-ball umpires just don't bother. OBR long prohibited touching the lips with the pitching hand or the ball while on the slope of the mound but finally revised it. Now, OBR, FED and NCAA all allow touching the pitching hand (only, not the ball) to the lips while off the rubber provided the pitcher immediately wipes off the fingers. The penalty is a ball added to the batter's count.

IV. THE FIELDERS

80. What's a catch?

Controlling the ball in hand or glove without the intentional use of anything else. With apologies to the otherwise excellent film *A League of Their Own*, a player purposely catching it in a cap has caught nothing but attention (Q&A 48). Once a ball touches anything but another defensive player, it's no catch.

What constitutes control? Time is a factor, and unlike football, the ground *can* cause a fumble. And, kid, if it pops out of your glove when you hold it up to show me you have control, you did *not* have control.

Control of a thrown ball only matters when an out is at stake; its lack is one reason a runner who seems out gets called safe. Another brings crowds to their feet shouting...

81. Whadaya mean, "missed the tag?"

Much like the strike zone, how can people possibly think they can evaluate a fast-unfolding tag play from the stands better than an umpire who's a few feet away and has no stake in the outcome? Please. Some umps keep the peace and keep up the pace with the if-the-ball-beats-you-you're-out theory, but others say there are three parts to a tag play: the throw, the catch, *and* the tag. Which theory is right? Whichever one the umpire chooses to use: these are *judgment* calls (Q&A **94**). *But*: if the runner is safe because the fielder tagged a left foot after the right foot hit the base or because the fielder laid the glove *on* the base rather than *in front* of it (scientific fact: if that sliding runner's foot is on the ground, it *will* touch base *before* glove), I *promise* you it won't look that way through the prisms of distance, angle, or team loyalty.

82. Is there a rule on how "high" you can tag a runner?

A rule? No, you heard an explanation. The feet of a five-foot-tall runner, sliding feet-first and tagged on or above the shoulders less than four feet from the base, *must* have hit the base before the tag. This is not about why the call was made—it was made because the umpire saw the runner touch the base before the tag—but about why it *looked* wrong from a distance.

83. What's a neighborhood call?

An "unwritten" rule, most often cited on the first out of a double play (Q&A 43) and throws to first: the fielder is clearly no longer touching the bag at the moment of the catch but the runner is called out. Well, why risk getting the fielder cleated if the play isn't close? This comes under the "if it doesn't make any difference, it doesn't make any difference" theory. However, if the throw *pulls* the fielder off, this does not apply.

84. How could you call that ball foul? That was in fair territory!

Depends which "that" you're saying was in fair territory. The player? Doesn't matter! The ball? You're right! This is decided *solely* on where *the ball* is when the fielder touches it. (Q&A 11)

85. How could you get between that batted ball and my kid?

How could I not? This is a for-real; I barely got out of the way of a screaming eagle right at me, and the shortstop couldn't make the play. I doubt he could have anyway—no reflection on him, it was a *screaming eagle*!

Shouting Daddy actually addressed his son, and not as a question. He obviously meant it for all ears including mine: "Don't let that umpire get between you and the ball! If he's in your way, you tell him to move!" Sound advice—if I'd been between batter and shortstop at the pitch. Ain't what happened; the screaming eagle was at *me*, not at the shortstop with me standing in between. This happens. I've been hit by fair batted balls twice in forty-plus seasons; it can't be prevented by pre-positioning, just quick reflexes. Even the batter doesn't know where the ball's going!

86. What's obstruction?

Not to be confused with interference (Q&As 24 and 54), this is an act by the defense that impedes a runner. The ump will kill the ball—right away if a play was being made on the obstructed runner, and if not then when the action stops—and award bases to offset the violation. This may be nothing, if the ump believes all runners got to where they would have.

Contact is not necessary, just making a runner slow down or even change direction! Standing in a base path or on a base impedes, and therefore obstructs, an approaching runner. We may also use this rule to penalize fielders for faking a tag without having the ball; making a player suddenly leave the feet not only impedes but endangers.

A player fielding a batted or thrown ball in the baseline is there legally, so just seeing a runner go around a fielder doesn't mean obstruction. You can also have contact and no obstruction—a collision between a fielder going for a thrown ball and a runner going for a base is often, as they say in basketball, incidental contact. "Incidental" doesn't mean slight, it means secondary to the action of the play.

87. What's this thing called the "Infield Fly Rule"?

Baseball's most misunderstood rule may be on your mind because of batter, runner, or fielder. It protects runners, so I explain it in **The Runner(s)** (Q&A 44). You may want to wait until this inning is over; it'll take some time.

88. The rule book says, "The line from home base through the pitcher's plate to second base shall run east–northeast." Why in the world does *that* matter?

Ask me again if your first baseman loses a throw in the sun.

V. THE UMPIRE(S)

89. What does everybody talk about when they get together at home plate before the game?

We tell jokes. (What's a two-base hit in the Alaska Baseball League? A double in tundra!)

Seriously, this get-acquainted/ground-rules session is crucial. These games are usually played in the same place, so everybody knows everybody and the local rules we call "ground rules." Still, we must verify this and that players are properly equipped. Local options—time limits, mercy rules, inning run limits, courtesy runners, whether to throw pitches on intentional walks—should be stated, if not for the teams' benefit then for ours. You'd be surprised at the variance, and we who work different leagues must be sure to know what rules are in play *that day*.

If there is a time limit, the start time must be noted. Unless a league stipulates otherwise, this is not the scheduled start time or when the first pitch is thrown but when the plate umpire calls "Play." Typically, time limits don't stop a game cold; they just say you can't start another inning. However, once the outcome is certain, the game should be stopped cold, just like not finishing the bottom of the last inning when the home team takes the lead. This *can* jar folks in the stands who don't know the rule or aren't paying attention: home team batting and leading, time limit hits, game over; score tied, home team batting, time limit hits, home team then scores, game over; home team leading, top of inning ends with so few minutes left you can't change sides and get three outs before time, game's over.

90. What officials' signals should I know?

A lot less than for football or basketball! I'll lay out more, but all you *really* need are strike/out/safe, and, wait a sec…

My right hand out front, fingers up and palm out, means *do not pitch*. (In FED, this is a dead ball—a difference that matters if there are runners and might be the basis for the myth in Q&A 50. Many umps insist it's dead in OBR, too, but nothing in the rules supports that and as you'll soon see the signal for time/ dead ball is BOTH hands up.) We retract it by beckoning or pointing toward the pitcher.

The right hand and arm indicate *strike* in one of several acceptable styles; there is no physical signal for *ball* unless the ump chooses to spot the miss with the *left* hand. (This, and verbalizations like "ball, low" are discouraged; one manual puts it "Call 'em, don't explain 'em.") A third strike adds a punching or sweeping motion such as the late Eric Gregg's "ripping the phone book." Although a *foul tip* is just like a strike (Q&A 15), it has its own signal: brushing the palm of the right hand across the back of the left. On a partial swing, when the plate umpire decides it was a swing, we point at the batter before making the strike sign. We indicate the number of balls and strikes (the *count*) vocally and/or digitally (um… fingers, not computers) or both. Balls precede strikes, so "2-and-1" means two balls/one strike; raised fingers on the left hand are balls with those on the right strikes. A 3-2 (or "full") count is often indicated by a fist rather than three left and two right fingers; higher-level umps *never* do this, but you'll see it a lot in amateur ball.

We indicate *out* with, like strike, our right arm and fist in one of several acceptable styles. Arms out from shoulders, palms down parallel with the ground, means *safe*—or, on an unsuccessful tag attempt on a player between bases with the play still in progress, not out (yet). Base umpires also use these to answer the plate ump's call for help on a half swing—*safe* meaning no swing, of course, and *out* meaning swing. The safe sign is also used to signal that a live ball near dead-ball territory is indeed alive and, after contact between players, no interference or obstruction.

Safe/out calls may be followed by a *why* sign, especially if the call is questioned. (These are explanatory and therefore used sparingly—remember, "Call 'em, don't explain 'em.") On a non-tag play, if the throw beat the runner but the fielder was off the bag, we follow the safe sign by sweeping both arms away from the bag. Following a safe sign by dropping our arms to our sides, raising one straight ahead from the shoulder, palm down, then lowering it and doing the same with the other arm—like the sign for double dribble in basketball—means the fielder didn't control the ball before the runner arrived. We indicate a dropped ball by pointing at it, or where it was before the fielder recovered it. Hands in front of the body, palms toward each other—like the martial-arts ready position—means no tag, the space between the hands implying "missed by that much." If we follow a tag play by tapping a part of our body, we're showing where the glove or ball touched the runner. This may follow either a safe or out call; after a safe, it means the tag was made there after the runner reached the bag; after an out, it shows where we saw a tag against a claim that the fielder didn't touch the runner.

On a close *fair/foul* call, we either silently point toward fair territory or fling both arms into the air, shout "Foul!" and point to foul ground. Some umps only shout foul on this, but the signal is important so everyone knows it *is* the ump who's shouting "foul." Silence on a fair ball, of course, is so no one mishears "foul" from "fair." Both arms in the air actually signals *dead ball* or *time*, but of course a foul *is* dead and that means time *is* out. This might seem confusing, but the clue is what else is happening when you see this signal: if the ball was just hit near a foul line, it means *foul*; if it was actively in play, it means *dead ball*; if neither, I'm just calling *time*. Also, we verbalize "foul," "dead ball," or "time" while giving the signal.

We signal *infield fly* by pointing at the ball in flight and making a verbal call that, unfortunately, often goes unheard amid cheering. It's often hard to convince players and coaches that we *did* call it, even though the rule specifically says an infield fly is an infield fly even if it went uncalled.

Right arm straight out from shoulder, fist clenched, is a *delayed dead ball.* You'll see this after a balk when the pitcher pitches or throws anyway, catcher's interference (Q&A 24) or possibly when a runner leaves too soon in a no-leadoff league that does not use flags (Q&A 62). *Obstruction*, which usually results in a delayed dead ball, is signaled with hands on hips, elbows out, like football's off-side signal.

There is no signal, as such, for *interference*; we simply point at the action and call, "That's interference!" This is a dead ball, so we follow that by so signaling and declaring outs and/or placement of runners we believe will offset the interference.

The *home run* signal is circling the right index finger above the head. If the ball went out near a foul pole or barely over the wall, or hit something beyond the playing field and bounced back in, we may precede this with some forceful pointing.

There are other signals. These are intended for us to communicate with each other, but what the heck. The plate umpire should be giving them, with base umpire(s) affirming them by repeating them. Touching the bill of the cap reminds an infield fly is possible. (I originally learned laying the right fist on the chest, which is still used in softball. I'm not sure if this changed over time or, as I moved around, with geography.) Laying the first two fingers of the right hand on top of the left wrist, where most people wear a watch, reminds of the possibility of a time play (Q&A 93). A base ump who taps the top of the cap, brushes the front of the jersey or waggles the fingers is asking the count of balls and strikes on the batter; pointing toward the ground asks how many are out. Other signals involving where we'll go if the ball is hit into the outfield—which we call "rotation"—are complicated and of no real use to you.

91. When is a ball alive, and when is it dead?

When the umpire calls "Play" (not "Play ball," which I suppose originated in some old movie), the ball is alive. This, or beckoning or pointing toward the pitcher, is done at the scheduled start time once all players are in position. Also, after any dead ball and after the pitcher is in position on the rubber (Q&A 50), these options resume play.

When the ball is dead, nothing can happen except to complete what happened while it was alive, like taking an awarded base. Ways the ball can become dead include an uncaught foul (one caught in the air is as alive as a fair fly, just as a foul tip is as alive as a swinging strike [Q&A 15]); a ball going into a dead-ball area; when pitched, hitting a batter; when batted, hitting any offensive player or umpire (usually, see Q&A 57); and any of the several kinds of interference.

The ball also becomes dead when an umpire calls "Time." (Baseball having no clock, it's strange that we use the word "time" to kill the ball; then again, people repeatedly shouting "Kill!" would be pretty morbid.) Barring "light failure or incapacitating injury," even we cannot call (or grant) time while a play is in progress.

92. What's "in progress?"

If no runner is trying to advance and the defense has the ball in the infield, we can grant time (that's the interpretation of the OBR wording "when no further play is possible"). The ball is then dead until the plate umpire calls "play" (but see Q&A 91), which we cannot do until, but should do as soon as, the pitcher takes position with the ball. Sharp runners often ask for time because it precludes the hidden ball trick, which can only be tried if someone other than the pitcher is holding a live baseball. That's one reason we may not grant every timeout request—is it *fair* to preclude the hidden ball trick?

93. Should I believe an ump who claims not to know the score?

Probably. Unless a run rule becomes a factor, the last thing I worry about is the score! The score doesn't affect whether a pitch is a ball or a strike or a runner is out or safe. Besides, nowadays most places have scoreboards.

Be aware the plate umpire, not the official scorer, decides whether a run counts. This only matters with a "time play"—a runner hits the plate just as the defense gets a third out elsewhere *on a non-force play* (by rule, no run can score during a force play that ends an inning). The ump points at the plate to score the run, or waves it off just as a basketball official tells everyone that last basket didn't count. This is *purely* a judgment call.

94. What's a judgment call?

A call that involves only judgment, no rule interpretation—out/safe, ball/strike, etc. By rule, a judgment call can*not* be argued. We'll discuss a call to some extent, but when the conversation unnecessarily delays the game or turns *uncivil*, we'll end it. If that requires an ejection, that's what it requires—even if I was wrong, there's no point arguing all day when the youngsters are there *to play*! We can check, at our discretion, with another ump and a coach can *ask* us to, but see Q&A 96. The only time we *must* check is on the appeal of a half swing (except FED; Q&A 30).

95. So you can never get a bad call overturned?

Not a bad *judgment* call—unless the umpire who made the call decides to confer with another ump. The rules *do* provide a procedure, called a "protest," for a team to press a claim that an umpire misapplied a rule. A protest must be lodged before the next pitch is delivered or runner is retired, or on game-ending plays within a specified length of time (OBR says by noon the next day). If the protesting team loses the game but wins the protest *and* the league decides the incorrect ruling impacted the outcome, the game will be replayed from how things stood at the time, which is why noses get buried in scorebooks when these arise. Again, this cannot be done on any judgment call, *only* when questioning an interpretation or application of a rule.

96. So umps do help each other?

Sure, but "getting help" is *solely* up to the umpire responsible for the call. OBR is *quite* explicit: "No umpire shall criticize, seek to reverse or interfere with another umpire's decision unless asked to do so by the umpire making it." (I guess my partner in Q&A 62 never read that.) Asking for help is not always as good an idea as it sounds, especially in the two-umpire system used in most amateur games. We must watch our jurisdiction first, but little looks worse to a fan than seeing one umpire check to another who was obviously looking elsewhere (where, before you come out of your seat, the consulted umpire was *supposed* to be looking!).

Still, we do work to be ready to help. Say the base umpire is perfectly positioned on a throw to first, but the throw is off the mark and the first baseman tries a swipe tag. From an otherwise perfect position, the base ump has a poor angle and a good chance of being blocked as to whether the glove touched the runner. Guess who has a perfect angle: the plate ump!

In no-leadoff leagues, base umpires must position themselves to see runner(s) and batter simultaneously to watch for leaving too soon. This means outside the base paths (Q&A 98), which may force us to call plays from behind, where it's also easy to be blocked from seeing a missed tag or a ball being dropped and quickly recovered. A partner can likely come to the rescue here, but in these and all cases except a half swing, it's up to the umpire responsible for the call whether to ask. Barring the unusual, I *had* the better view; that's why it's my call! That, not wanting to make my partner guess, is the reason we don't ask; it isn't pride.

If I had the correct angle and a good view, I'm sure I'm right. That's not ego; it's the job! As for pride, all umps worth their counters would rather be right than proud!

97. Would you admit it if you were *sure* you saw another umpire miss a call?

Only with other umpires, and then only to discuss what went wrong so it won't happen again.

98. So, any pointers on telling a good umpire from a bad one?

Indeed—and they might take away my union card for this too—many.

Appearance is a dead giveaway. Sloppy uniform? Poor umpire! The cap is *never* worn backward, like a catcher's; the short-billed cap that's designed for plate work fits very well inside the mask. Unimportant as it may seem, plate-brushing technique is a great sign—briskly but thorough comes *only* with practice. No ball bag should ever hang on a base ump's belt; only the plate umpire should keep spare baseballs.

Watch what blue's doing between innings. Hurrying players (nicely), counting warm-up pitches, tossing in a new baseball if a warm-up pitch gets away, arranging spare baseballs so the best ones will be used next, talking mechanics with the partner(s), or standing quietly on a foul line.

Calling plays quickly is *not* a good thing; *the objective is to call it right, not fast.* The great Bill Klem, who pretty much invented umpiring as we know it today—working over the catcher's shoulder, the inside chest protector, plate signals—said, "It ain't nothin' 'til I call it." When I wait a beat before calling a pitch, I'm much less likely to want to take that call back, which of course I *must not* do. Taking time before calling a foul is just being careful; "FOUL!" kills the ball and so cannot be corrected. Waiting before calling a tag play lets us make sure the fielder has or retains control of the ball. This can seem indecisive, but it's actually superb mechanics—a certain sign of experience. (So you'll forgive us for having very little patience with a coach shouting "Who called that?" if someone on the other team "beats" us to a call.) These delays shouldn't vary; the ump who takes the same amount of time before making each call—especially on pitches—is, as players would say, "*really* in the zone." Who's *not* in the zone? The umpire whose time between catch and call *does* vary or whose call mixes with or even precedes the sound of ball striking leather.

A plate umpire (officially, "umpire-in-chief") will use one of several acceptable stances, so you can't tell a lot from that. I feel too immobile on a knee, but many good umpires work that way. Watch the head, which must be stock-still at the pitch. The mask should always be on the face or in the *left* hand. Unless it's the hockey-style mask, it must come off to call a play versus a pitch, for the wider field of vision needed, but holding it in the right hand means whipping this fairly heavy object around to make a sign. We should even *remove* it with the left hand, which is tough for new umpires because their counter is in that hand. For more than twenty years, I confess, I didn't even try to do this correctly because I was certain that, as the hardest of hard-wired right-handers, I simply couldn't. I pulled it off with my right and handed it to myself, so to speak, by passing it to my left. But it's easier to drop it doing that than if you never change hands, plus I occasionally had a play develop so quickly that I couldn't switch hands before the call. One day, I decided to *try* the left, and it took some getting used to—for about two innings! Now I'd feel silly taking it off with my right hand, as I should have all along.

When the mask is off, the plate umpire must hold on to it! You want to get rid of it—especially the many umps who are former catchers—but a catcher has a reason: to make a play, not watch one to call it, so distraction is only an issue for the catcher. Let a catcher innocently toss a mask aside and another player trip over it, or the ball hit it or get in or under it, well, that's baseball; but let any of that happen with *my* mask and I've created an ugly interference situation.

The plate umpire should examine a returned baseball before putting it back in play or in the ball bag. (In the pros, balls are tossed out as "unfit" almost any time they touch dirt and as many as six dozen get used per game, but in our levels we try to get through on what we started with. That's usually four—not four dozen, four—maybe six. We rarely throw a ball out unless it's cut; if we use more it's because balls fouled out of the field weren't returned.) Anytime any ball becomes dead, or even gets more than two or three steps behind the catcher when there are no runners, I put in a different one; I and the catcher want on-deck hitters to retrieve balls not from laziness but to save time. Speaking of time, enforcing rules discussed in Q&A 75 would vastly streamline the game; why don't we? Because players and coaches hate it. It's *their* game; take that up with them!

For the base umpire (officially, the "field umpire"), positioning is very revealing in the two-umpire system most often used in amateur ball. With no runners, the correct spot is position A, just outside the right-field foul line. How far beyond first base is a triangulation: at least several feet past the bag, behind the first baseman's peripheral vision (no matter how deep), with a sight line to watch the pitcher for certain balks. With a runner only at first, it's position B: halfway between the mound and second base on an imaginary line from the plate through the first-base edge of the mound (in no-leadoff leagues, between the right-side infielders but behind *their* peripheral vision in shallow right field). With runner(s) anywhere else, it's position C: the same relative spot as B on the third-base side (same no-leadoff adjustment to short left). If you're lucky enough to see a three- or four-person crew, position D is the same spot relative to third base as A is to first. There are never five umpires, but there may be six; the extra two along the outfield foul lines for views of catch/no catch and fence-busting fly balls that are otherwise just not possible.

When the pitcher is ready, the base umpire(s) should be in the HOKS (hands on knees stance), leaning forward.

Watch for the "umpire pivot." If a field umpire is in position A, a hit into the outfield will bring that ump racing into the infield. A good one turns squarely to first base as the batter-runner reaches it, pausing for a good look at the touch of the bag.

There's great temptation for a base ump to get close. Close is good, but the priorities are angle and stillness. If we're moving at the moment that we call it, we have erred even if we get it right; bouncing eyeballs *absolutely* can be fooled. What we call "stop… lock…look…call it" is the *only* right way. Distance is not *nearly* as important as angle. In fact, watch a good base ump react to a pick-off try to first from positions B or C. As counterintuitive as it is, the correct step is toward home, not first, because the right angle to that tag play is toward the mound. (Counterintuitive? After forty-plus years, I still had trouble with this.)

We can get *too* close, especially on non-tag plays on which we watch runner and fielder and *listen* for ball to hit glove. I'll *never* forget a real bang-bang play at first (those are fun!) when I rang up the runner when the ball beat him by a blink. Trouble was, the bill of my cap had kept me from seeing the high throw I heard hit the glove bounce off of it. I changed the call immediately—the one situation in which we can and should, because it's a correction based on new information rather than a change of mind—but if I'd been a step back or waited a beat, I wouldn't have had to.

Watch and listen for umpires to communicate with each other. In the two-umpire system, almost any call except ball/strike, fair/foul inside the bags, or fair/foul to left field can be either's jurisdiction depending on the situation at time of the pitch and/or how the play develops. This would take more explanation than can fit into this volume—as would explaining the systems. Rule books say field umpires may stand wherever we believe will give us the best view, but we *do* have systems—one for crews of one, two, three, four or six umpires working games with leadoffs and a whole other set for all five crew sizes in games without. These systems are complex and sophisticated. Explaining them would make *this* an umpire manual, but it's fair to say, and for you to know, that if two umpires call the same play (even if they make the same call, at great relief to both) or if neither calls a play, then somebody has made a mistake; but which ump calls that play at third base or whether that tagging runner left early just depends.

Speaking of jurisdictions, *only* the plate umpire (again, really "umpire-in-chief") can declare a forfeit. However, *any* ump can eject (technically, "disqualify;" our slang is "run" or "dump") any team personnel any time, including before or after the game.

Plays should be viewed and called from a right angle, but there are right angles and then there are right angles. For example, we get head-on to tag plays at the plate because if it's close the runner will twist to avoid the tag and that twist presents a right angle. What if it isn't close? Why, then, it isn't close; you can call that from the stands, right?

Enthusiasm is good, but the line between enthusiasm and showboating is thin. Umps who bellow *every* out or strike call are either rookies or showboats. On out/safe, we lay it on thick only when it's close (which we call "selling the call"). On the plate, some umps don't verbalize a ball at all, even though manuals advise saying "ball" loudly enough for infielders' ears. As for strikes: rookies, showboat and actors in movies with poor technical advice may voice-call them all, but a veteran umpire says nothing on a swinging strike. Make a strike sign, sure, but everybody saw the batter swing. Exception: on an unsuccessfully checked swing, most plate umpires will say something like "Yes, you did" while making the strike sign. As for how loudly to call strikes, manuals suggest escalating from one to two and again to three. You may have noticed that some of us are pretty flamboyant when calling a third strike, but we should *not* be when that fatal strike was by swinging.

Close foul calls, though, *should* be done loudly. Well-coached players run until they hear "foul," so we should make sure they can, in fact, hear it. (Don't get any ideas, defense—yelling "foul" on a fair ball is obstruction, unsportsmanlike conduct, and anything else I can think up.)

Finally, please note I never mentioned…the thumb. It isn't used for any sign—not outs, not ejections, not anything.

99. Why would an umpire refuse to sweep the plate?

Oh, you were there that night?

Look, sweeping the plate in a drizzle only makes it blend in with the mud around it. In this situation, I might use my shoe or the *handle* of my plate brush to scrape the corners, which is all I really need anyway. What's more, no one else needs the plate at all. Think about it: the pitcher's target is the catcher's mitt, and the hitter's is the ball!

100. Speaking of rain, what if the ump wants to play on and I think they should stop? My kid's out there!

Hey, so am I! Once the game starts, this is solely up to the plate umpire; only safety supersedes getting the game in.

This question is usually asked about lightning, but before we go there, let me point out that we often play on in a drizzle that's not making it hard to see the ball or making the field too slippery. Fact is, a player is much more likely to get hurt slipping on a wet surface—especially home plate, but also the base bags and, of course, grass—than from lightning. That said, I'll keep when to stop as simple as possible by addressing only lightning from here on.

I was lucky enough to umpire with a guy who was then closing in on forty years as a National Weather Service meteorologist; naturally, I asked his advice. He told me, "Get 'em off the field if you see streak, but if you only see flash, count Mississippis until you hear thunder. If you reach five, play on." I followed that until the NWS had big-leaguer Torii Hunter tell us all, "If you hear thunder, get indoors." Now, I suspect—given contrary advice from such an *extremely* qualified source—that this campaign overreaches toward the safe side. However, it's simpler, known to the public, easy to apply consistently, and credible to parents; I can live with it. I apply it literally, though; if I see lightning but don't hear thunder—so-called "heat lightning"—we're playing on. Also, I can tell you from attending hundreds of professional games that the pros themselves are not taking Torii's advice.

It's easy but impractical to say "get 'em off the field" if you see any lightning at all. Look, lightning can be visible for almost a hundred miles, rarely strikes more than ten, has *never* been proven to have struck even fifty–and yet, from the near edge of a storm that's too far away for you to see, can actually strike from a seemingly clear sky. I know what you're thinking: "What are the chances of that?" Admittedly slim, but *you're* chasing a *zero* chance of being struck. Given *all* the facts, the only way to reach zero is: *never* do *any*thing *any*where outside *ever* again. Hey, I'm a parent, too—*and* as at-risk as *anyone* on the field! You *can* pull *your* child, of course; that's between you, your kid, your conscience and the coach. It only involves the umpire if it forces a forfeit. And by the way, if it comes to that point the umpire will have not one single choice; if you leave too few players behind, I can do nothing but declare the forfeit.

When we do stop a game for weather, we can't legally call it immediately. We can only suspend it, because the rules say we must wait thirty minutes before calling a game for "weather or condition of the playing field." I say "legally"—our fields usually have no tarps, so common sense often prevails as rain makes rivers in the infield.

101. What if I've read all this, and I *still* hate this ump?

That's your privilege. It's now mine to quote OBR one more time: "Each umpire has authority to rule on any point not specifically covered in these rules."

Maybe *one* more: "No umpire may be replaced during a game unless he is injured or becomes ill."

VI. THE LAST CALL

Umpires are people, too! Sure, the verbal abuse described in the Introduction goes with the territory, but that doesn't make it right. You don't talk to the pizza delivery guy that way even if your order *is* screwed up. With literally hundreds of calls every game, even if the four or five you didn't like were all wrong, that's still a pretty good average. Most of you only notice the "bad" calls with which you disagree, and it's no coincidence that they are almost always those that go against your team.

At pro games, I hear yells of, "Do your job!" You know, when you say that in everyday life, you're asking for adequacy; to an umpire, you're demanding perfection against a standard measured to your completely nonobjective and often under-informed perception!

You only needed to get 70 percent of your test answers right to get through school, right? Training, in most people's work, has that same standard. Well, the last umpiring test I took required 90. Yet when I make a single mistake, as of course I have, I've heard everything from "pitiful" to "worst ever." For one call. (Although, I may say, I've never *actually* heard anyone yell "Kill the umpire!" at me.)

A quote floating around the game says umpiring is "the only profession where you have to be perfect on day 1 and get better from there." I don't know who first said that, but here behind the mask it rings pretty true.

So how would you like to have a big crowd of people watching you at your work, judging and loudly commenting on your every move all day? You'd want a wire fence too, wouldn't you?

www.ingramcontent.com/pod-product-compliance
Lightning Source LLC
Chambersburg PA
CBHW062018040426
42447CB00010B/2058